C000180167

Stella Maidment and Lorena Rob

Class Book

1

OXFORD
UNIVERSITY PRESS

The school

Mr Potter

Miss Davis

The shop

HAPPY STREET SCHOOL

Jason

BUS STOP

The park

Daisy

Mum

1

Welcome to Happy Street!

Come and play at our house!
Come and play today!
I'm Polly.
And I'm Jack!
My name's Greg.
Hello, Greg!
Hello, hello, hello, hello!
Come and play today!

4

7 **Sing the song.**

A game in the garden – one, two,
A game in the garden – three.
A game in the garden – four, five,
Give the ball to me.

A game in the garden – six, seven,
A game in the garden – eight.
A game in the garden – nine, ten,
Hurry! I can't wait.

One, two, three, four, five, six,
Seven, eight, nine, ten.
Knock the skittles over,
And start the game again.

8 **Listen and point.**

one	two	three	four	five	six	seven	eight	nine	ten

6

Read.

2 At school

Say the chant.

HAPPY STREET SCHOOL

Look! What's this?
It's a pencil, a pencil!
Hey, Greg!
Your pencil!
Pick it up now!

12 **Listen and point.**

| a pencil | a pen | a rubber | a ruler | a pencil-case | a book |

8

Listen and read.

Show me something red, red!
  Here is something red, red!

Show me something blue, blue!
  Here is something blue, blue!

Show me something green, green!
  Here is something green, green!

Show me something yellow too!
  Here is something yellow too!

17 **Listen and point.**

red   blue   green   yellow   black   brown   orange   pink   white   purple

10

Listen and repeat.

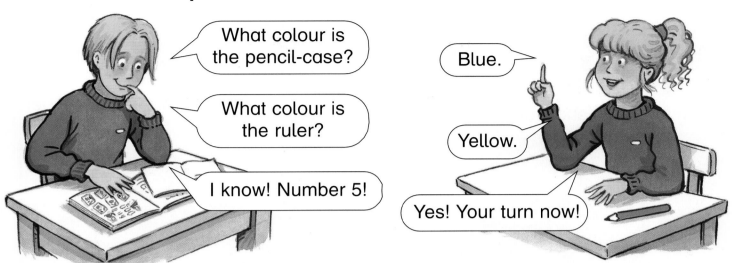

👥 **Now play the game.**

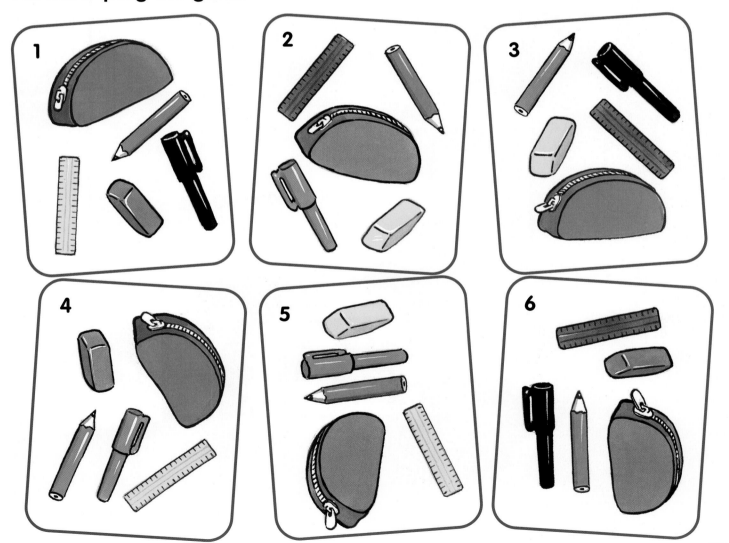

Read.

Colin in Computerland

Story 1: The Red Dragon

Who's this?

Knock! Knock! Knock!

What's your name?

Er... I'm Colin.

OK. Here you are!

What's this? A torch and a computer game! Great!

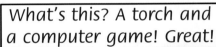

Two, three, two, three, two?

OK, two... three... two... three... two...

WOOOOAAAAAAH!

End of part 1...

3. At Happy House

Sing the song.

Playing with a car
On the playroom floor.
Listen! Can you hear
A dinosaur roar?

25 **Listen and point.**

a car   a doll   a robot   a train   a lorry   a dinosaur

14

1. What's this? Is it a car?

   No. Wait and see!

2. I know! It's a robot!

3. Is it a robot, Daisy?

   I don't know!

4. Is it a robot, Jack?

   No, it isn't!

5. It isn't a car… and it isn't a robot… hmm.

6. Is it a rocket, Polly?

   Yes, it is! It's a rocket!

7. 10, 9, 8, 7, 6, 5, 4, 3, 2, 1 *BLAST OFF!*

29 **Say the chant.**

1

I'm a red robot – tell me what to do!
I'm a blue robot – tell me what to do!

Red robot – stand up!
Blue robot – stand up!

2

Chorus
Red robot – hands up!
Blue robot – hands up!

3

Chorus
Red robot – hands down!
Blue robot – hands down!

4

Chorus
Red robot – turn around!
Blue robot – turn around!

5

Chorus
Red robot – touch your head!
Blue robot – touch your head!

6

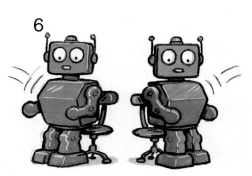

Red robot – sit down!
Blue robot – sit down!

16

31 **Listen and repeat.**

👥 **Now play the game.**

Read.

Colin in Computerland

The Red Dragon: Part 2

All about me!

Read the letter.

9 Park Street
London

5th May

Dear Peter,
Hello, I'm Holly! I'm your new penfriend.
I'm eight and I'm from London. I've got
a brother and two sisters. I like gymnastics,
pop music, and animals.

I've got lots of pets – a dog, two cats,
and a rabbit. When I grow up I want
to be a vet.

What about you? Have you got any pets?
What do you want to be when you
grow up?

Write soon,

Love,

Holly

This is my brother Harry, and my sisters – Ann and Charlotte.

Gymnastics is my favourite sport.

This is me and my rabbit, Benjamin.

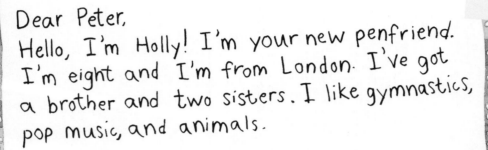

Now write a letter to your penfriend – all about you.

When I grow up I want to be …

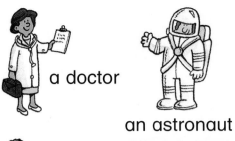
a doctor

an astronaut

a singer

a teacher

a racing-driver

a dancer

a vet

a nurse

Say the rhyme.

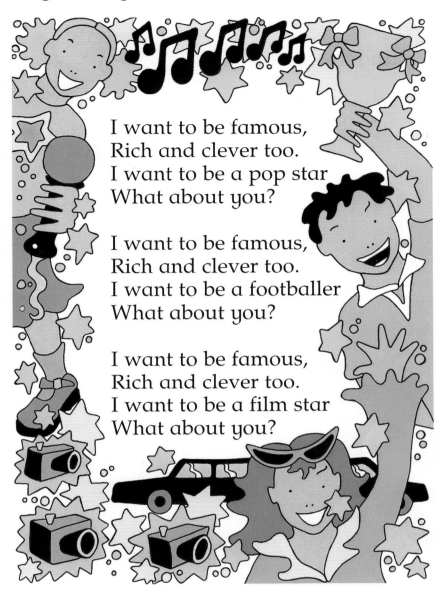

I want to be famous,
Rich and clever too.
I want to be a pop star
What about you?

I want to be famous,
Rich and clever too.
I want to be a footballer
What about you?

I want to be famous,
Rich and clever too.
I want to be a film star
What about you?

Fun with Fred!

4 At the shop

38 **Say the chant.**

Do you want an apple?
An apple for your tea?
Or do you want an ice cream?
An ice cream, please!

39 **Listen and point.**

an apple   an orange   a cake   a pear   a banana   an ice cream

Listen and read.

I like pizzas, I like steak,
I like pasta too.
I like cats – cats are great!
But no, I don't like you!
MIAOW!

I like biscuits, I like cakes,
I like chocolate too.
I like dogs – dogs are great!
But no, I don't like you!
GRRRRR!

24

Listen and repeat.

mushrooms

olives

peppers

Do you like mushrooms?

Do you like olives?

Do you like peppers?

You want pizza number 2!

Yes!

No!

Yes!

Yes!

Now play the game.

Pizza Menu

1

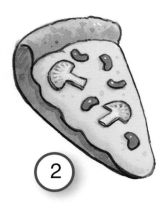
2

3

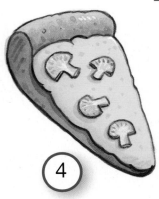
4

5

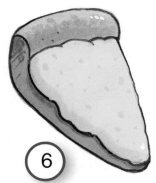
6

7

8

Read.

I like cereal and milk for breakfast.

My favourite lunch is hamburger and chips.

I like chocolate cake and orange juice for tea.

26

Colin in Computerland

The Red Dragon: Part 3

End of part 3...

5 At the park

50 Sing the song.

I've got a ball,
I've got a ball,
I've got a ball,
Now let's go!
Let's go to the park!
Let's go to the park!

51 Listen and point.

a ball   a kite   a plane   a boat   a bike   a skateboard

[55] **Say the chant.**

Hide and seek! Hide and seek!
Close your eyes and please don't peek!
Count to twenty – slowly please!
Open your eyes – you can't find me!

1, 2, 3, 4,
5, 6, 7, 8,
9, 10, 11, 12,
13, 14, 15, 16,
17, 18, 19, 20.
Coming to find you!

30

Listen and repeat.

Have you got a big red kite?

Have you got a big blue ball?

Have you got a small brown boat?

Aha! You're… Bob!

No, I haven't.

Yes, I have.

Yes, I have.

Now play the game.

1

Joe

2

Sally

3

Bob

4

Helen

5

Tom

6

Tina

Read.

I haven't got a tennis racket and I haven't got a ball!

That's OK! I've got two tennis rackets and lots of balls! Let's play tennis!

Look – I've got rollerblades.

I've got rollerblades too! Let's have a race!

Colin in Computerland

The Red Dragon: Part 4

Party time!

Read about Tom's birthday wish.

1

Marcia: Happy Birthday, Tom.
Tom: Thank you!
Marcia: How old are you, Tom?
Tom: Well, count the candles.
Marcia: OK! One, two, three, four, five, six, seven, eight… There are eight candles.
Tom: Yes, that's right. I'm eight today.

2

Marcia: Well, go on, Tom! Close your eyes, blow out the candles, and make a wish!
Tom: A wish?
Marcia: Yes. When it's your birthday you can make a wish and it will come true. Try it!
Tom: OK! I wish for… a magic horse!

3

Children: Wow! Look! A magic horse…
Marcia: Yes. It can fly – look, it's got wings!
Unicorn: Happy birthday, Tom.
Children: And it can talk!
Unicorn: Climb on my back, Tom. Come for a ride!

4

Unicorn: Hold on tight, Tom. One, two three… Go!
Tom: Bye, everyone!
Children: Bye, Tom!
Marcia: You see… a birthday wish can come true!

Make a wish for your birthday.

Read the rhyme. Then play the party game.

1 The farmer's in his den
  The farmer's in his den
  E – I E – I
  The farmer's in his den.

2 The farmer wants a wife…

3 The wife wants a child…

4 The child wants a dog…

5 We all pat the dog…

dog   farmer   wife   child

The farmer's in his den…

The farmer wants a wife…

We all pat the dog…

Fun with Fred!

Happy Birthday to you! I went to the zoo.

I saw a big monkey…

And I thought it was you!

6 Greg's flat

Sing the song.

Feathers on the table!
Feathers on the chair!
Feathers on the bookcase!
Feathers everywhere!
Oh Greg! Oh Greg!

Feathers on the cupboard!
Feathers on the bed!
Feathers on the wardrobe!
Feathers on your head!
Oh Greg! Oh Greg!

64 **Listen and point.**

| a table | a chair | a bookcase | a cupboard | a bed | a wardrobe |

Listen and read.

68 **Sing the song.**

1 Flossy's got a ball.
  Flossy's got a ball.
  Rolling, rolling, rolling. Woof!
  Flossy's got a ball.

2 Now I'm in the kitchen,
  Mmm – nice smell! *Chorus*

3 Now I'm in the bathroom,
  Yuck! I'm wet! *Chorus*

4 Now I'm in the sitting room,
  Oh, please play! *Chorus*

5 Now I'm in the bedroom,
  Phew! I'm tired!

6 Rolling, rolling, rolling… Stop!
  Flossy's got a ball.

38

Listen and repeat.

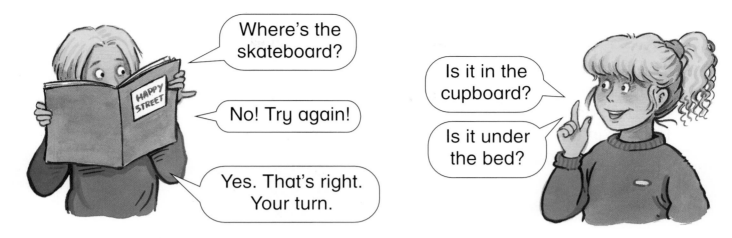

Now play the game.

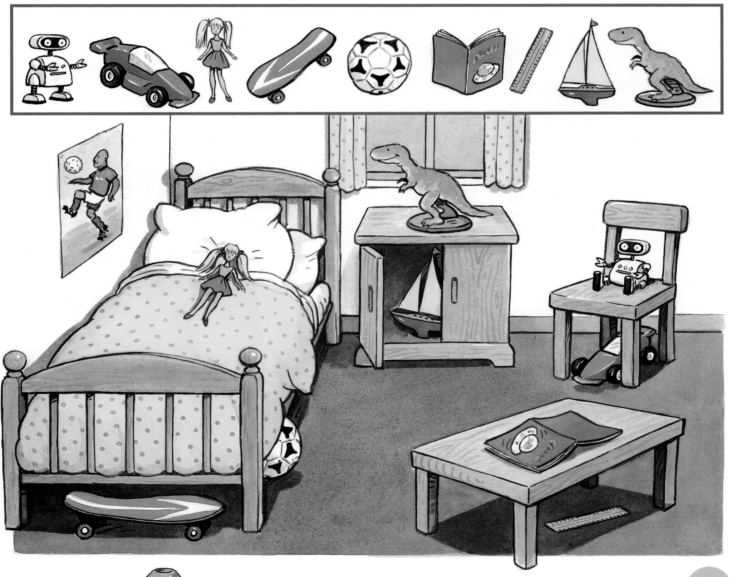

Read.

Come and see my bedroom! There's a computer on the table. There's a guitar under the bed, and there's a toy box in the cupboard. I like my bedroom. It's great!

Colin in Computerland

Story 2: The Gold Robber

7. In the street

Sing the song.

A woman and a dog
Waiting at the bus stop.
A woman and a dog
Waiting at the bus stop.

A boy and a baby
Waiting at the bus stop.
A boy and a baby
　And a woman and a dog
Waiting at the bus stop.

A man and a girl
Waiting at the bus stop.
A man and a girl
　And a boy and a baby
　　And a woman and a dog
Waiting at the bus stop.

78 **Listen and point.**

a woman	a dog	a boy	a baby	a man	a girl

42

 **Listen and read.**

1 Now, where's my friend Pam?

2 No, Pam's got long brown hair.

Is that Pam?

3 Look, she's got long brown hair.

Sssh Jack! He's a man!

4 SHE'S got long hair!

Yes, she's got long BLACK hair. Pam's got long BROWN hair!

5 SHE'S got long brown hair!

Don't be silly, Jack!

6 Hello, Pam! I like your hair!

Thank you!

7 But she's got short blond hair!

Sing the song.

Tall and short,
Tall and short,
Everybody's out in the street!

Fat and thin,
Fat and thin,
Everybody's out in the street!

Old and young,
Old and young,
Everybody's out in the street!

Everybody's out in the morning sun.
Everybody's out in the street!

44

Listen and repeat.

He's a boy. He's tall and he's got brown hair.

Yes.

That's right – your turn now!

A boy… and he's tall, and he's got brown hair.

I know. Number 4!

Now play the game.

Unit 7 Lesson 4

Read.

My best friend is called John. He's short and he's got short blond hair. He's got blue eyes. Can you see him?

My best friend is called Helena. She's tall and she's got long red hair. She's got blue eyes. Can you see her?

Colin in Computerland

The Gold Robber: Part 2

Home sweet home

Read about these houses.

This boy lives in a flat in the city. It's quite small, but it's got big windows, a balcony, and a beautiful view over the park.

This girl lives on a houseboat on the river. It's called 'Rosie Lee'. It's red and black and yellow. It hasn't got a garden, but it's got lots of flowers.

This woman lives in a cottage in the country. It's very small – it's got two rooms upstairs and two rooms downstairs! It's got a roof made of straw.

This man lives in an old windmill. All the rooms are round! It's got one big room on each floor and lots of stairs.

What's your home like?

48

Say the poem and frighten your friend.

It's dark in the street –
but don't be afraid!
Look all around –
there's a house!

It's dark in the house –
but don't be afraid!
Look all around –
there's a cupboard.

It's dark in the cupboard –
but don't be afraid!
Look all around –
there's a box.

It's dark in the box –
but don't be afraid!
Look all around –
there's a . . .

MOUSE!

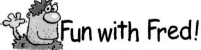

8 In the playground

Sing the song.

I'm muddy! There's mud on my T-shirt.
There's mud on my socks and my shoes.
I'm muddy! There's mud on my trousers.
I've got the muddy boy blues!

I'm muddy! There's mud on my jumper.
There's mud on my socks and my shoes.
I'm muddy! There's mud on my skirt.
I've got the muddy girl blues!

90 **Listen and point.**

| a T-shirt | socks | shoes | trousers | a jumper | a skirt |

Listen and read.

1 Jumpers… shoes… socks… dear, dear!

2 Now, this is Polly's jumper. Here you are, Polly.

Thank you, Miss Davis!

3 And this is Greg's shoe!

Thank you, Miss Davis!

4 And whose hat is this? Jack?

I don't know!

5 Oh good! There's my hat! Thank you, Miss Davis!

6 It's Mr Potter's hat!

Unit 8 Lesson 2

Sing the song.

I don't like this jumper,
  this jumper, this jumper,
I don't like this jumper.
This jumper's too big.

  Then put on another, another, another,
  Then put on another, another, dear Greg!

I don't like this jumper,
  this jumper, this jumper,
I don't like this jumper.
This jumper's too small.

  Then put on another, another, another,
  Then put on another, another, dear Greg!

I love this jumper,
  this jumper, this jumper,
I love this jumper.
This jumper's just right!

 **Listen and repeat.**

Now play the game.

Read.

It's my birthday party. I'm wearing red trousers and Dad's white shirt and I've got a sword. I'm a pirate!

I'm wearing a long dress and I've got a necklace. I'm a princess and I've got a crown!

I'm a cat. I'm wearing a black T-shirt, a black skirt, and black tights. I've got a long black tail!

My trousers are too big and my hat is too small. I'm a clown!

Colin in Computerland

The Gold Robber: Part 3

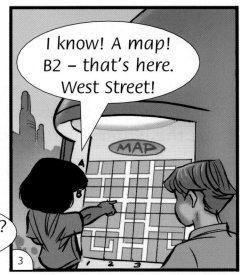

End of part 3…

9 At the sports centre

101 **Say the chant.**

My feet are in the water
And I'm feeling brave and bold.
My feet are in the water
But the water's very cold!

My legs are in the water...

My body's in the water...

My arms are in the water...

My hands are in the water...

My head is in the water
And I'm feeling brave and bold,
My head is in the water...

102 **Listen and point.**

| a foot | a leg | a body | an arm | a hand | a head |

104 **Listen and read.**

Unit 9 Lesson 2

57

106 **Say the chant.**

1 Arms up!

2 Arms down!

3 Jump to the right!

4 Jump to the left!

5 Kick to the right!

6 Kick to the left!

7 Hands on hips!

8 Bend to the right!

9 Bend to the left!

10 And… rest!

58

Listen and repeat.

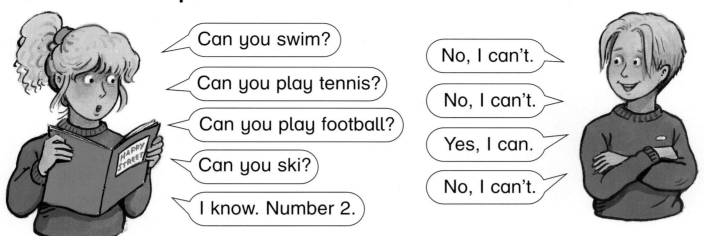

Can you swim?

Can you play tennis?

Can you play football?

Can you ski?

I know. Number 2.

No, I can't.

No, I can't.

Yes, I can.

No, I can't.

Now play the game.

Read.

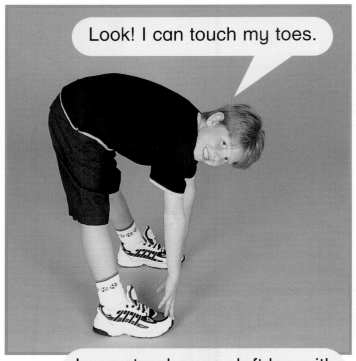

Look! I can touch my toes.

I can touch my head with my foot.

I can stand on my left leg with my right hand on my head.

I can rub my tummy and pat my head.

Colin in Computerland

The Gold Robber: Part 4

In disguise

a beard

glasses

a moustache

earrings

sunglasses

a hat

Can you help find the Turner Twins?

WANTED

TWIN BANK ROBBERS
Jane and Johnny Turner –
always in disguise!

Read the detectives' reports…
BUT BE CAREFUL!
Detective Darcy's report is RIGHT
BUT
Detective Biggle's report is WRONG!

TOP SECRET

Report on: The Turner Twins
By: Detective Dave Darcy
Date: 13th January

The bank robbers, Jane and Johnny Turner, are in the airport.

They've got three million pounds in a blue bag.

I think Jane's wearing sunglasses and I think she's got long hair. I think Johnny's got black hair and a moustache.

We must catch them!

Dave Darcy

TOP SECRET

Report on: The Turner Twins
By: Detective Eric Biggle
Date: 13th January

I think Jane and Johnny Turner are in the airport.

They've got three million pounds in a green bag.

I think Jane's got brown hair and big earrings. I think Johnny's got a beard and I think he's wearing glasses.

We must catch them!

Eric Biggle

Describe another person in the airport for your friend to find.

UNIVERSITY PRESS

Great Clarendon Street, Oxford OX2 6DP

Oxford University Press is a department of the University of Oxford. It furthers the University's objective of excellence in research, scholarship, and education by publishing worldwide in

Oxford New York

Athens Auckland Bangkok Bogotá Buenos Aires Calcutta
Cape Town Chennai Dar es Salaam Delhi Florence
Hong Kong Istanbul Karachi Kuala Lumpur Madrid
Melbourne Mexico City Mumbai Nairobi Paris São Paulo
Singapore Taipei Tokyo Toronto Warsaw

with associated companies in Berlin Ibadan

Oxford and Oxford English are registered trade marks of Oxford University Press in the UK and in certain other countries

© Oxford University Press 2000

The moral rights of the authors have been asserted

Database right Oxford University Press

First published 2000

No unauthorized photocopying

All rights reserved. No part of this publication may be reproduced, stored in a retrieval system, or transmitted, in any form or by any means, without the prior permission in writing of Oxford University Press, or as expressly permitted by law, or under terms agreed with the appropriate reprographics rights organization. Enquiries concerning reproduction outside the scope of the above should be sent to the ELT Rights Department, Oxford University Press, at the address above

You must not circulate this book in any other binding or cover and you must impose the same condition on any acquirer

ISBN 0 19 4338339

2000 Impression

Printed in Hong Kong

Acknowledgements
The authors and publishers would like to thank all the teachers who have contributed so usefully to the development of the project at all stages of its development.

Illustrations
Happy Street characters and artwork by Peter Stevenson
Colin in Computerland by Peter Richardson

Garry Davies pp 21 (occupations), 62, 63; Kelly Harrison pp 21 (rhyme), 35; Anna Leplar Elizabeth Roy Literary Agency p 34; Bernice Lum (Quizzy and Ziggy); Claire Mumford p 49; Jim Peacock pp 21, 35, 49, 63 (Fun with Fred); Mark Ruffle p 20 (handwriting)

Commissioned photography
Haddon Davies pp 48 (portraits), 62
Sandi Friend pp 7, 12, 18, 26, 32, 40, 46, 54, 60

The publishers would like to thank the following for permission to reproduce photographs:
Collections pp 20 (girl with pet rabbit/Sandra Lousada), 48 (apartment block/Lesley Howling, windmill/Gill Jones, thatched cottage/Liz Stares); Sally & Richard Greenhill p 48 (house boat); Popperfoto p 20 (gymnast/Dave Joiner); Janine Wiedel p 20 (boy and girls)

We would like to thank the following for their help:
Cycle King, Oxford; Furniture Village plc, Abingdon; Thames Valley Systems plc, Reading